LITTLE CRITTER READING

Grade 2

Table of Contents

Columbus, Ohio

Credits:

School Specialty Children's Publishing Editorial/Production Team

Vincent F. Douglas, B.S. and M. Ed.

Tracey E. Dils

Jennifer Blashkiw Pawley

Teresa A. Domnauer

Tracy R. Paulus

Suzanne M. Diehm

Big Tuna Trading Company Art/Editorial/Production Team

Mercer Mayer

John R. Sansevere

Erica Farber

Brian MacMullen

Matthew Rossetti

Billy Steers

Diane Dubreuil

Atomic Age, Inc.

Send all inquiries to:
School Specialty Children's Publishing
8720 Orion Place
Columbus, OH 43240-2111

ISBN 0-7696-3022-7

2 3 4 5 6 7 8 9 10 POH 09 08 07 06 05 04

WELCOME TO CRITTERVILLE!

Spider

Frog

Grasshopper

Mouse

Little Critter

Little Sister

Dad

Kitty

Mom

Dog

Gator

Bat Child

Gabby

Bun Bun

Tiger

Maurice

Molly

Malcolm

Trouble With Blue

Read to see why Little Critter has to clean up the garden.

1 Little Critter saw his mom standing at the door of his room. "Mom, why are you holding a shovel?" asked Little Critter.

2 "I think you will need it, Little Critter," said Mrs. Critter.

3 "Why?" asked Little Critter.

4 "Come downstairs and see," said Little Sister, poking her head inside.

5 Little Critter followed his mom and sister out to the yard. The garden was a mess!

6 "Oh, no!" said Little Critter. "Blue's been digging again."

7 "Little Critter," said Mrs. Critter, "I think Blue needs to be trained."

8 "You're right, Mom," agreed Little Critter. "I better train him. It shouldn't be hard. Blue is smart."

9 Blue barked and wagged his tail. Little Sister giggled as she looked at Blue's muddy paws. "He doesn't look very smart to me!"

Knowing the Words

Write the story words that have these meanings.

1. a tool that scoops

____
(Par. 1)

2. place where plants grow

____
(Par. 5)

3. taught

____
(Par. 7)

Reading and Thinking

1. This story is mostly about

_____ Little Critter's room.

_____ a problem with Blue.

_____ a problem with Little Sister.

Words such as **he**, **she**, and **it** take the place of other words. Read these sentences. Then fill in the blanks.

Little Critter shouted as he ran.
He stands for Little Critter.

2. Her mom laughed as she talked.
She stands for ____________.

3. My dad talked as he worked.
He stands for ____________.

Blue Gets Out

Read to find out where Blue goes.

1 The next day, Little Critter's mom asked him to get the mail.

2 "Sure, Mom," answered Little Critter. He walked down the path to the mailbox. He unlatched the gate, opened the mailbox, and got the mail. On his way back to the house, he looked at the mail.

3 Just then Blue saw the open gate. He dashed past Little Critter and ran out of the yard. "Blue, come back!" cried Little Critter. "Here, Blue!" Little Critter dropped the mail and chased his dog.

4 Blue jumped over a fence. Little Critter jumped over the fence. Blue crawled under some bushes. Little Critter crawled under the bushes. He could not catch Blue. Little Critter ran through his neighbors' yards and called for Blue. He ran right into Mrs. Crabtree.

5 "I'm sorry, Mrs. Crabtree. I was just looking for..." Little Critter tried to explain.

6 Mrs. Crabtree frowned. "I think I know just who you are looking for," she said.

Knowing the Words

Write the story words that have these meanings.

1. place for mail

_______________ (Par. 2)

2. ran after

_______________ (Par. 3)

3. made an unhappy face

_______________ (Par. 6)

Reading and Thinking

1. What is the name of Little Critter's neighbor?

____

Why do you think she was frowning?

____

____

2. What happened first in the story? Put **1** by it. What happened next? Put **2** by it. Put **3** by the thing that happened last.

_____ Little Critter chased Blue.

_____ Little Critter ran into Mrs. Crabtree.

_____ Little Critter went to get the mail.

Gabby's Idea

Read to see what the friends plan.

1 A little while later, Gabby came over to Little Critter's house with a big sign. It read: Lemonade — five cents a cup.

2 "My idea is to open a lemonade stand," said Gabby. "Then we can sell lemonade to make money."

3 "Great idea," said Little Critter. "I'll make the lemonade."

4 "Maurice and I will get paper cups," said Molly.

5 "I'll bring a table and chairs," added Tiger.

6 "Meet you here in half an hour," said Gabby.

7 Little Critter hurried to make the lemonade. The directions said to use two scoops of lemonade mix, but Little Critter used four. He wanted to make sure it tasted really good.

8 Little Critter carried the heavy pitcher outside. "We're ready for business!" he said.

Reading and Thinking

Some of these sentences are about **real** things, things that could happen. Write **R** by them. The other sentences are about things that could not happen, **make-believe** things. Write **M** by them.

1. ______ A dog can run and play.
2. ______ A house can talk.
3. ______ A dog likes bones.
4. ______ A dog likes to read.
5. What was Gabby's idea? ______

____

Learning to Study

Write each set of words in A-B-C order.

1. cups table lemonade

____

____

____

2. chairs idea house

____

____

____

3. later sign money

____

____

____

More Trouble for Blue

Read to see what happens at the lemonade stand.

1 Little Critter and his friends sat at the lemonade stand. Blue lay on the ground at Little Critter's feet and chewed on Little Critter's shoelaces.

2 Just then Su Su walked by with her dog, Fifi. Fifi had pink ribbons in her curly white fur. She smelled like perfume.

3 "Do you want some lemonade, Su Su?" asked Little Critter. "It's only five cents a cup."

4 "Okay," said Su Su. Suddenly, Blue bounded over to Fifi and began to sniff her. The two dogs started to play. Blue ran to the garden and began to dig. Fifi pulled on her leash, trying to follow him.

5 "Stop that right now, Fifi!" ordered Su Su. Fifi wouldn't listen. She pulled so hard, Su Su lost hold of the leash. Fifi ran after Blue.

6 "Here, Fifi!" cried Su Su.

7 "Here, Blue!" called Little Critter. The dogs wouldn't listen. They just kept playing in the dirt.

8 "Fifi is a purebred poodle," Su Su yelled at Little Critter. "And I'm training her for the dog show. I knew I shouldn't let her play with a mutt, like your dog."

9 Su Su stomped off and dragged Fifi out of the dirt. Her ribbons had come untied. Her white fur was all brown.

10 "Oh, no, Blue," said Little Critter. "More trouble."

Reading and Thinking

Put each word in the right blank.

walked pulled sniffed

1. Blue ____________ Fifi.
2. Su Su ____________ with Fifi.
3. Fifi ____________ on the leash.

Write **R** by the sentences that are about **real** things. Write **M** by the sentences about **make-believe** things.

4. _____ Dogs can make lemonade.
5. _____ People can make lemonade.
6. _____ People put ice in lemonade.
7. _____ Ice keeps drinks warm.

Working With Words

A **base** word is a word without an ending. The words in each row have the same **base** word. Circle the ending of each one. Then write the **base** word in the blank.

1. playing
   played
   plays
   ____

2. starting
   started
   starts
   ____

Circle the best word for each sentence. Then write it in the blank.

3. We'll eat ____________ he comes.
   then when check

4. Please finish ____________ apples.
   chase those shoes

Little Critter's News

Read to find out if Little Critter's mom and dad like the news.

1 Little Critter ran home with Little Sister and Blue. "Mom! Dad!" he called, as he opened the door. "Guess what? We're going to enter Blue in the dog show! First prize is twenty-five dollars. If Blue wins, then I can pay Mrs. Crabtree the money I owe her."

2 "Good idea," said Mr. Critter. Mrs. Critter thought so, too.

3 Little Sister shook her head. "How are you going to train him if he never listens?" she asked.

4 "Learning to listen is part of the training, Little Sister," said Mrs. Critter. "We have to remember Blue is just a puppy. He can learn."

5 Suddenly, Blue started whining. The Critters saw a puddle on the floor right next to him.

6 "Little Critter, I think Blue needs to go out," said Mr. Critter.

7 "He sure has a lot to learn," said Little Sister.

Reading and Thinking

Look at each picture and circle the sentence that goes with it.

1. Blue is playing outside.

   Blue is playing in the house.

2. Blue sleeps on Little Critter's bed.

   Blue sleeps in his doghouse.

3. What did Mr. Critter say about the dog show? ______________________________

4. What will Little Critter do if Blue wins the dog show? ______________________________

5. What did Little Sister say about Blue? ______________________________

Working With Words

Circle the best word for each sentence. Then write it in the blank.

1. Blue has a ______________.

   tan   than   tail

2. Blue can win a ______________.

   prize   quiet   paint

3. The floor was ______________.

   pet   met   wet

Write these sentences. Use one of the shorter words from the box to stand for the words that are underlined.

We'll	isn't	can't	didn't	I'm

4. <u>We will</u> be there.

   ____

5. He <u>did not</u> go.

   ____

6. The puppy <u>is not</u> hurt.

   ____

7. <u>I am</u> hungry.

   ____

8. Blue <u>cannot</u> do tricks.

   ____

Blue's First Lesson

Read to see how much Blue has to learn.

1 Gabby, Maurice, Molly, and Tiger all came over to Little Critter's house to help train Blue. Gabby brought her dog training book, *Dog Training the Easy Way.*

2 "I don't think there is an easy way to train Blue," said Little Sister. Maurice and Molly laughed.

3 "Lesson One: Teach Your Dog His Name," Gabby read aloud. "Always use your dog's name when you ask him to do something."

4 "Here, Blue!" Gabby called. Blue jumped up and licked Gabby's face. "You try, Little Critter," she said, as she wiped her face.

5 "Here, Blue!" said Little Critter. Blue jumped on Little Critter and knocked him down. "You try, Tiger," he said.

6 "Here, Blue!" shouted Tiger. Blue bounded toward him and grabbed the baseball out of his hand. Then he ran for the garden with the ball in his mouth.

7 "We're finished with Lesson One," said Gabby. "Blue definitely knows his name."

8 "That's about all he knows," said Little Sister.

Reading and Thinking

1. This story is mostly about

    _____ Tiger's ball.

    _____ Gabby's dog.

    _____ Blue's first lesson.

Fill in the blanks.

2. Little Critter said, "good dog," as he petted Blue.

    He stands for ______________.

3. Gabby brought her book and put it on the table.

    It stands for ______________.

Working With Words

Circle the best word for each sentence. Then write it in the blank.

1. The lesson is too ______________.

    leg   long   log

2. The dog's eyes are ______________.

    big   bag   buy

3. Gabby told Blue to ______________.

    sat   set   sit

4. They have a ______________ pet.

    now   not   new

Read these words and look at the pictures.

Gabby's friend

her friend's hand

You can see that you add **'s** when you want to show that the hand belongs to Little Critter. Now write these names the same way.

5. Little Critter ______________ hand

6. Gabby ______________ hand

Mrs. Crabtree Stops By

Read to find out what Mrs. Crabtree has to say about the dog show.

1 Gabby came to train Blue every afternoon. No matter how hard Little Critter and his friends worked, Blue still did not listen.

2 One afternoon, when Little Critter was working with Blue, Mrs. Crabtree came over. "Sit, Blue!" said Little Critter. Blue kept rolling around in the grass instead.

3 "Hello!" said Mrs. Crabtree. She looked at Little Critter, then at Blue, and back again. "What are you kids up to?"

4 "Hi, Mrs. Crabtree," said Little Critter. "We're training Blue for the dog show. First prize is twenty-five dollars. If Blue wins, then I can pay you for the roses."

5 "Really?" asked Mrs. Crabtree, looking down at Blue. He was digging a hole at her feet.

6 Little Critter smiled at Mrs. Crabtree. He put his arms around Blue.

7 "Good luck!" said Mrs. Crabtree, frowning.

8 "Good luck!" repeated Little Sister. "You're definitely going to need it!"

Reading and Thinking

1. This story is mostly about

    _____ Mrs. Crabtree's roses.

    _____ Mrs. Crabtree's visit.

    _____ Mrs. Crabtree's feet.

2. Instead of sitting, Blue ______________

    ______________________________.

3. Why do you think Mrs. Crabtree came over? ______________

Working With Words

Circle the best word for each sentence. Then write it in the blank.

1. Mrs. Crabtree ______________ over.

    stayed came ate

2. I see you ______________ every day.

    her help here

3. I ______________ to brush my dog.

    little like let

Read these words and look at the pictures.

dog

dogs

You can see that you add **s** to show that you mean more than one dog. Write these words so that they mean more than one.

4. rose ______________

5. friend ______________

6. lesson ______________

The Dog Show

Read to see what the show dogs do.

1 The next morning, Little Critter put the new collar on Blue. He took off the T-shirt. Then he said, "Blue, I know you can be the winner." The Critter family got Blue into the car with no problems. They drove to the park.

2 Many people were already at the park to watch the dog show. Little Critter's friends were there to cheer for Blue.

3 "Good luck, Blue!" said Gabby and Tiger.

4 Maurice and Molly said, "We brought some hot dogs, just in case."

5 Little Critter watched the other dogs. He began to get nervous. Blue was number eight. After a while, Su Su and Fifi took their turn. Fifi wore a pink sweater with matching bows. She did all her tricks with no mistakes. Su Su smiled proudly when Fifi was finished.

6 The next dog took his turn. He was a beagle named Scout. Scout's owner had Scout sit, heel, speak, and roll over. Scout stood up on two legs and danced. Then he did a back flip. Finally, Scout carried a flower to the judges. Everyone clapped for Scout, even Su Su. It was Blue's turn next. Little Critter headed to the ring.

7 Mr. and Mrs. Critter wished Little Critter good luck.

8 Tiger and Little Sister shouted, "Go, Blue! Blue is number one!"

Reading and Thinking

Put each word in the right blank.

collar clapped brought

1. Little Critter put a new ________ on Blue.

2. Maurice and Molly ________ hot dogs.

3. Everyone ________ for Scout.

4. This story is mostly about

____ what the dogs do at the dog show.

____ what Tiger does at the dog show.

____ what Little Sister does at the dog show.

Working With Words

To make a word mean more than one, add **-es** if the word ends in **s**, **ss**, **ch**, **sh**, or **x**. Write these words so that they mean more than one.

1. lunch ________
2. dish ________
3. box ________

Fill in the missing letter so the sentence makes sense.

4. I like to h___lp my dad.
5. Blue j___mped on Little Critter.
6. Little Critter p___cked up the ball.

Fill in the missing letters so each sentence makes sense.

ar or ur

7. Soon it will be Blue's t___n.
8. Can we play in the p___k?

Sweet Dreams for Little Critter and Blue

Read to see why everyone is happy.

1 Mrs. Crabtree thanked Little Critter and his friends for all their hard work. She was very happy about her rose garden. Her whole yard looked beautiful. "Thank you, too, Blue," she said and petted him. "You're a good dog."

2 "Good-bye, Mrs. Crabtree!" said all the friends.

3 Little Critter and Little Sister headed home. "I'm glad Mrs. Crabtree is our friend," said Little Critter. "I think she even likes Blue now."

4 "I think you're right," said Little Sister.

5 "Woof! Woof!" barked Blue.

6 After dinner, Little Critter went out to the doghouse. He brought Blue some dog food and some fresh water. They sat inside the doghouse together. "You know what, Blue?" said Little Critter. "You're the best dog in the whole wide world!" Little Critter yawned and put his arm around Blue.

7 Soon, Little Critter and Blue were fast asleep. Little Critter dreamed of gold coins and roses. Blue dreamed of hot dogs and digging.

Reading and Thinking

1. What did Little Critter say to Blue?

____

____

Fill in the blanks.

2. Tiger and Gabby talked as they worked.
   They stands for _______________

   ____

3. Mrs. Crabtree answered, and she said, "Yes, Little Critter."
   She stands for _______________

   ____

Working With Words

The missing word in each sentence sounds like **new**. Change the **n** in **new** to **bl**, **fl**, and **thr**. Write the new words, and put them in the right sentences.

1. ________ ________ ________

2. The wind ________ hard.

3. I ________ my dog a ball.

4. The bird ________ away.

Circle the best word for each sentence. Then write it in the blank.

5. Little Critter will ________ Blue.
   grass brush growl

6. Will Maurice and Molly ________ with us?
   dry play fry

The ending **-er** means "more" and the ending **-est** means "most." Add the endings **-er** and **-est** to these base words.

	-er	**-est**
clean	cleaner	cleanest
7. kind	________	________
8. fast	________	________

What Will Little Critter Do at the Farm?

Read to see what Little Critter wants to do at the farm.

1 Mrs. Critter helped Little Critter pack his bag. She said, "Choose two of your favorite things to bring." Little Critter picked his cowboy boots and his teddy bear.

2 "Little Critter, we can put your bicycle on the back of the car, but you won't need your football helmet and skateboard at the farm."

3 "Okay, Mom. Grandpa and I will have lots to do anyway. We can go fishing, play baseball, ride the horses, and play checkers."

4 "Little Critter, you will have fun, but don't forget that a farm is a busy place. Grandma and Grandpa have a lot to do every day. Maybe you could help," said Mrs. Critter.

5 "Yes, I can help!" said Little Critter.

6 Little Sister popped into the room. "I can help, too! I want to go to the farm, too!"

7 Mrs. Critter said, "Little Sister, this time it's Little Critter's turn to visit. Next time it will be your turn. You will do fun things here at home."

8 "But I want my turn now!" said Little Sister.

9 Mr. Critter called upstairs, "Okay, everyone to bed early tonight. We have a long drive tomorrow!"

Knowing the Words

Write the words from the story that have these meanings.

1. thing you like best ______________ (Par. 1)

2. to take ______________ (Par. 1)

3. must have ______________ (Par. 2)

The words **come** and **go** have meanings so different that they are **opposite.** Make a line from each word in the first list to the word in the second list with the opposite meaning.

4. early	front
5. long	short
6. back	late

Working With Words

A word without any ending is a **base word.** The base word of **talking** is **talk.** Circle each base word below.

1. picks   2. helped   3. playing

Sometimes one word stands for two words. The word **didn't** stands for **did not.** Write a word from the story that can stand for each pair of words.

4. do not ______________ (Par. 4)

5. it is ______________ (Par. 7)

Reading and Thinking

1. Check the answer that tells what the story is mostly about.
   - ______ Little Critter's teddy bear
   - ______ what Little Critter will do at the farm
   - ______ Little Sister's bicycle

2. What did Mrs. Critter help Little Critter do? ______________

   ____

3. Check the sentence that tells what Little Sister wanted.
   - ______ to play checkers
   - ______ to go fishing
   - ______ to go to the farm

4. Why did Mrs. Critter say Little Critter would not need his football helmet and skateboard?

   ____

   ____

   ____

Cooling Off

Read to see how Grandpa and Little Critter cool off.

1 After feeding the pigs, the chickens, and the turkeys, Little Critter and Grandpa put on their swimsuits.

2 "A little dip in the water will cool us off," said Grandpa. They walked down the hill to the pond. They put their towels down on the grass. Butterflies floated around the pond, and crickets chirped. The sun sparkled on the water.

3 Little Critter stuck his toe in the pond. A frog leaped over his foot. Little Critter jumped back. He looked down and saw tiny fish swimming around.

4 "You go in first, Grandpa," said Little Critter.

5 "Oh, frogs and fish won't hurt you, Little Critter," said Grandpa. "Maybe one day this week we can come down here and do some fishing."

6 "That would be great! I love fishing!" said Little Critter.

7 Grandpa jumped in the water and swam around. Little Critter paddled around after him. The cool water felt wonderful on such a hot, sticky day. They swam for just a few minutes.

8 "Well, Little Critter, I'm afraid that's all the time we have. Let's dry off, eat some lunch, and get back to work."

Knowing the Words

Words that mean the same or nearly the same are called **synonyms.** Use lines to match synonyms.

1. little	quick
2. close	tiny
3. fast	near

Working With Words

A **compound word** is made by putting two words together. Write a compound word for the underlined words below. One is done for you.

A word meaning <u>some</u> kind of <u>thing</u> is ___something___.

1. A <u>suit</u> to <u>swim</u> in is a

_______________.

2. A time <u>after</u> the <u>noon</u> time is

_______________.

Fill in each blank with the right pair of letters to make a word.

ch sh th wh

3. ____ey	6. ____irped
4. lun____	7. fi____
5. ____eel	8. su____

Reading and Thinking

1. What was Little Critter afraid of?

____

Write **R** by the real things. Write **M** by the make-believe things.

2. ____ Frogs can fly.
3. ____ Crickets chirp.
4. ____ Fish wear swimsuits.
5. ____ Butterflies fly.

6. Check the answer that tells what time of year it is in the story.

____ fall

____ summer

____ winter

The Critter Country Fair

Read to see what is going on at the fair.

1 It was a hot, bright summer morning. Little Critter and his grandparents headed for the Critter Country Fair.

2 When they arrived, Little Critter looked all around. The rides whirled. The animals *mooed* and *crowed* and *baaed* in the barns. Music played loudly. Fair workers called out to come play their games. There were contests to show off garden vegetables, fresh-baked pies, and homemade jars of jelly. The warm air smelled of sweet cotton candy and spicy mustard.

3 Grandma needed to bring their pie to the cooking tent. The pie would be kept in a cool place until it was time for the contest.

4 "What should we do, Little Critter?" asked Grandpa, as he wiped his brow.

5 "Let's play a game, Grandpa!" said Little Critter. "Let's play that game where you spray water in the clown's mouth and blow up a balloon."

6 Little Critter and Grandpa sat down at the game. Little Critter held his sprayer tightly and aimed at the clown's mouth. He turned to talk to Grandpa when suddenly the game began! Little Critter sprayed water all over Grandpa's shirt instead of in the clown's mouth.

7 "Well, Little Critter, that's one way to cool off!" said Grandpa.

Knowing the Words

In each row, circle two words that have opposite meanings.

1. see	close	far	look
2. never	few	always	some
3. cry	break	sleep	wake

Working With Words

A word part that can be said by itself is called a **syllable.** Some words have two consonants between two vowels. These words can be divided between the consonants, as in **pic|nic.** In each word below, draw a line to divide the word into syllables.

1. s u m m e r
2. s u d d e n
3. c o t t o n
4. c o n t e s t

Walk and **talk** are **rhyming words.** In rhyming words, only the beginning sound is different. Write words that rhyme with **spray** by changing **spr** in **spray** to **p** or **w.**

5. ____________ 6. ____________

Then use each new word in the right sentence.

7. Grandpa will show you the ________ to the fair.
8. We must ____________________ for our tickets.

Reading and Thinking

1. Check the answer that tells what the story is mostly about.
   _____ the pie contest
   _____ cotton candy
   _____ the fair

Write the best word to finish each sentence below.

2. I want to play that ______________ with Grandpa. (warm, game, tent)
3. Little Critter looked all ____________ the fair. (around, above, behind)
4. The clown had a bright red ______________________________. (jelly, garden, mouth)

Read these sentences. Then fill in the blanks.

5. Grandpa sneezed as he played the game.
   He stands for ________________.
6. Grandma heard music as she walked by the tent.
   She stands for ________________.
7. The ice cream melted as it sat on the table.
   It stands for ________________.

A Picnic for Dinner

Read to find out who would pack a healthier picnic.

1 "Grandma, are you making peanut butter and pickle sandwiches?" asked Little Critter.

2 "No, not today, Little Critter. These are chicken sandwiches. I thought we could go on a picnic for dinner tonight," said Grandma.

3 "A picnic! I love picnics!" said Little Critter.

4 Grandma and Grandpa and Little Critter walked to the apple orchard. There were rows and rows of trees filled with small green apples.

5 "Can we eat these apples, Grandma?" asked Little Critter.

6 "Not yet. They won't be ready until the fall," she said.

7 Grandpa spread out the picnic blanket. Grandma put the picnic basket on the blanket.

8 Grandma had packed chicken sandwiches, coleslaw, carrot sticks, strawberries, and some oatmeal cookies for dessert.

9 "Next time I can pack the picnic for you, Grandma," said Little Critter. "I'll bring brownies, potato chips, popcorn, cupcakes, and some soda pop. Oh yeah, and some peanut butter and pickle sandwiches."

10 Grandma and Grandpa grinned at each other.

11 "Don't you worry, Little Critter. Grandma is always glad to pack the picnic!" said Grandpa. "She has a knack for putting together a balanced meal."

12 "I sure do!" said Grandma. "Now eat your sandwich, Little Critter."

Knowing the Words

Circle the three words in each row that belong together.

1. apples	oranges	cats	bananas
2. chicken	dog	turkey	peacock
3. cookie	cake	candy	pizza
4. cake	water	milk	juice

Working With Words

Write the best word to finish each sentence below.

1. The class will ____________ for the bird. (care car)

2. Did someone ____________ dinner? (barn burn)

Most words add -**s** or -**es** to show more than one. Words that end in **y** are different. In most words that end in **y**, change the **y** to **i**, and add -**es**. Change the words below to mean more than one. One is done for you.

berry ____berries____

3. story ____________

4. penny ____________

5. puppy ____________

6. library ____________

Reading and Thinking

1. Check the answer that tells what the story is mostly about.

____ a picnic

____ eating apples

____ peanut butter and pickle sandwiches

2. Why couldn't Little Critter eat the apples?

____

____

____

3. Why is Grandma's picnic a "balanced" meal?

____

____

4. What would you pack for a healthy picnic?

____

____

5. Check three answers that are healthy snacks.

____ potato chips

____ strawberries

____ carrot sticks

____ candy

____ raisins

Words You Know

1.	2.	3.
run sun fun	friend faster flower	big birds ball
4.	**5.**	**6.**
dog did don't	pond play day	puppy cup sun
7.	**8.**	**9.**
to too two	fish frog butterfly	go game give
10.	**11.**	**12.**
hot not now	goes grass good	three there them
13.	**14.**	**15.**
yellow yard yes	be big bee	could come cold

Word Recognition (1-15): Have your child name each picture and circle the word that names or best describes the picture.

Knowing the Words

Write the story words that have these meanings.

1. a tool that scoops
shovel

2. place where plants grow
garden

3. taught
trained

Reading and Thinking

1. This story is mostly about
___ Little Critter's room.
✓ a problem with Blue.
___ a problem with Little Sister.

Words such as **he**, **she**, and **it** take the place of other words. Read these sentences. Then fill in the blanks.

Little Critter shouted as he ran.
He stands for Little Critter

2. Her mom laughed as she talked.
She stands for her mom

3. My dad talked as he worked.
He stands for my dad

Page 5

Knowing the Words

Write the story words that have these meanings.

1. place for mail
mailbox

2. ran after
chased

3. made an unhappy face
frowned

Reading and Thinking

1. What is the name of Little Critter's neighbor?
Mrs. Crabtree

Why do you think she was frowning?
Answers will vary. Example:
Because Blue ran in her yard.

2. What happened first in the story? Put **1** by it. What happened next? Put **2** by it. Put **3** by the thing that happened last.

2 Little Critter chased Blue.
3 Little Critter ran into Mrs. Crabtree.
1 Little Critter went to get the mail.

Page 7

Reading and Thinking

Some of these sentences are about **real** things, things that could happen. Write **R** by them. The other sentences are about things that could not happen, **make-believe** things. Write **M** by them.

1. R A dog can run and play.
2. M A house can talk.
3. R A dog likes bones.
4. M A dog likes to read.
5. What was Gabby's idea? to sell lemonade

Learning to Study

Write each set of words in A-B-C order.

1. cups table lemonade
cups
lemonade
table

2. chairs idea house
chairs
house
idea

3. later sign money
later
money
sign

Page 9

Reading and Thinking

Put each word in the right blank.

walked pulled sniffed

1. Blue sniffed Fifi.
2. Su Su walked with Fifi.
3. Fifi pulled on the leash.

Write **R** by the sentences that are about real things. Write **M** by the sentences about make-believe things.

4. M Dogs can make lemonade.
5. R People can make lemonade.
6. R People put ice in lemonade.
7. M Ice keeps drinks warm.

Working With Words

A base word is a word without an ending. The words in each row have the same **base** word. Circle the ending of each one. Then write the base word in the blank.

1. playing
played
plays
play

2. starting
started
starts
start

Circle the best word for each sentence. Then write it in the blank.

3. We'll eat when he comes.
then when check

4. Please finish those apples.
chase those shoes

Page 11

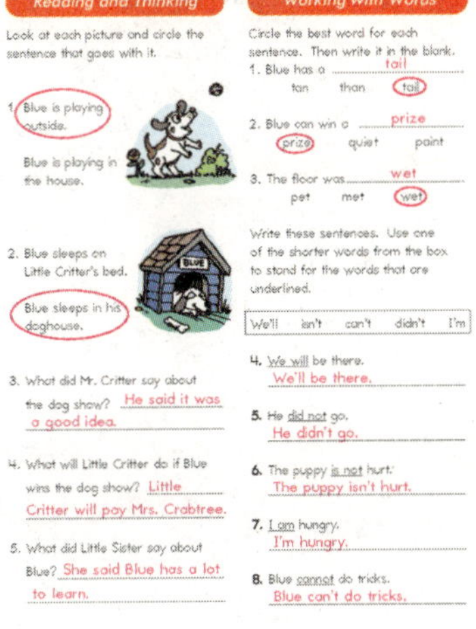

Reading and Thinking

Look at each picture and circle the sentence that goes with it.

1. Blue is playing outside.
Blue is playing in the house.

2. Blue sleeps on Little Critter's bed.
Blue sleeps in his doghouse.

3. What did Mr. Critter say about the dog show? He said it was a good idea.

4. What will Little Critter do if Blue wins the dog show? Little Critter will pay Mrs. Crabtree.

5. What did Little Sister say about Blue? She said Blue has a lot to learn.

Working With Words

Circle the best word for each sentence. Then write it in the blank.

1. Blue has a tail
tan than tail

2. Blue can win a prize
prize quiet paint

3. The floor was wet
pet met wet

Write these sentences. Use one of the shorter words from the box to stand for the words that are underlined.

We'll	isn't	can't	didn't	I'm

4. We will be there.
We'll be there.

5. He did not go.
He didn't go.

6. The puppy is not hurt.
The puppy isn't hurt.

7. I am hungry.
I'm hungry.

8. Blue cannot do tricks.
Blue can't do tricks.

Page 13

Reading and Thinking

1. This story is mostly about
___ Tiger's ball.
___ Gabby's dog.
✓ Blue's first lesson.

Fill in the blanks.

2. Little Critter said, "good dog," as he petted Blue.
He stands for Little Critter

3. Gabby brought her book and put it on the table.
It stands for her book

Working With Words

Circle the best word for each sentence. Then write it in the blank.

1. The lesson is too long
leg long log

2. The dog's eyes are big
big bag buy

3. Gabby told Blue to sit
sat set sit

4. They have a new pet.
now not new

Read these words and look at the pictures.

Gabby's friend
her friend's hand

You can see that you add **'s** when you want to show that the hand belongs to Little Critter. Now write these names the same way.

5. Little Critter Little Critter's hand
6. Gabby Gabby's hand

Page 15

Reading and Thinking

1. This story is mostly about
___ Mrs. Crabtree's roses.
✓ Mrs. Crabtree's visit.
___ Mrs. Crabtree's feet.

2. Instead of sitting, Blue rolled around in the grass.

3. Why do you think Mrs. Crabtree came over? Answers will vary.

Working With Words

Circle the best word for each sentence. Then write it in the blank.

1. Mrs. Crabtree came over.
stayed came ate

2. I see you here every day.
her help here

3. I like to brush my dog.
little like let

Read these words and look at the pictures.

dog
dogs

You can see that you add **s** to show that you mean more than one dog. Write these words so that they mean more than one.

4. rose roses
5. friend friends
6. lesson lessons

Page 17

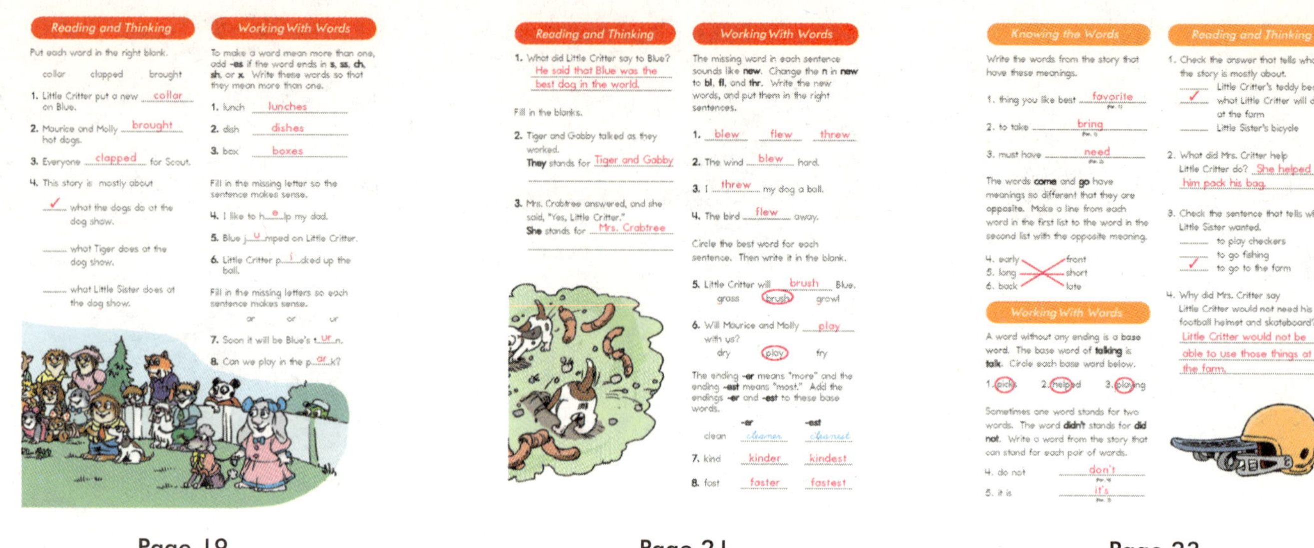

Reading and Thinking

Put each word in the right blank.

collar clapped brought

1. Little Critter put a new collar on Blue.
2. Maurice and Molly brought hot dogs.
3. Everyone clapped for Scout.
4. This story is mostly about
   - ✓ what the dogs do at the dog show.
   - what Tiger does at the dog show.
   - what Little Sister does at the dog show.

Working With Words

To make a word mean more than one, add **-es** if the word ends in **s, ss, ch, sh,** or **x**. Write these words so that they mean more than one.

1. lunch — lunches
2. dish — dishes
3. box — boxes

Fill in the missing letter so the sentence makes sense.

4. I like to h e lp my dad.
5. Blue j u mped on Little Critter.
6. Little Critter p i cked up the ball.

Fill in the missing letters so each sentence makes sense.

or ar ur

7. Soon it will be Blue's t ur n.
8. Can we play in the p ar k?

Page 19

Reading and Thinking

1. What did Little Critter say to Blue? He said that Blue was the best dog in the world.

Fill in the blanks.

2. Tiger and Gabby talked as they worked. **They** stands for Tiger and Gabby
3. Mrs. Crabtree answered, and she said, "Yes, Little Critter." **She** stands for Mrs. Crabtree

Working With Words

The missing word in each sentence sounds like **new**. Change the **n** in **new** to **bl, fl,** and **thr**. Write the new words, and put them in the right sentences.

1. blew flew threw
2. The wind blew hard.
3. I threw my dog a ball.
4. The bird flew away.

Circle the best word for each sentence. Then write it in the blank.

5. Little Critter will brush Blue. grass (brush) growl
6. Will Maurice and Molly play with us? dry (play) fry

The ending **-er** means "more" and the ending **-est** means "most." Add the endings **-er** and **-est** to these base words.

	-er	-est
clean	cleaner	cleanest
7. kind	kinder	kindest
8. fast	faster	fastest

Page 21

Knowing the Words

Write the words from the story that have these meanings.

1. thing you like best favorite
2. to take bring
3. must have need

The words **come** and **go** have meanings so different that they are opposite. Make a line from each word in the first list to the word in the second list with the opposite meaning.

4. early — late
5. long — short
6. back — front

Working With Words

A word without any ending is a base word. The base word of **talking** is **talk**. Circle each base word below.

1. (pick)s 2. (help)ed 3. (play)ing

Sometimes one word stands for two words. The word **didn't** stands for **did not**. Write a word from the story that can stand for each pair of words.

4. do not don't
5. it is it's

Reading and Thinking

1. Check the answer that tells what the story is mostly about.
   - Little Critter's teddy bear
   - ✓ what Little Critter will do at the farm
   - Little Sister's bicycle
2. What did Mrs. Critter help Little Critter do? She helped him pack his bag.
3. Check the sentence that tells what Little Sister wanted.
   - to play checkers
   - to go fishing
   - ✓ to go to the farm
4. Why did Mrs. Critter say Little Critter would not need his football helmet and skateboard? Little Critter would not be able to use those things at the farm.

Page 23

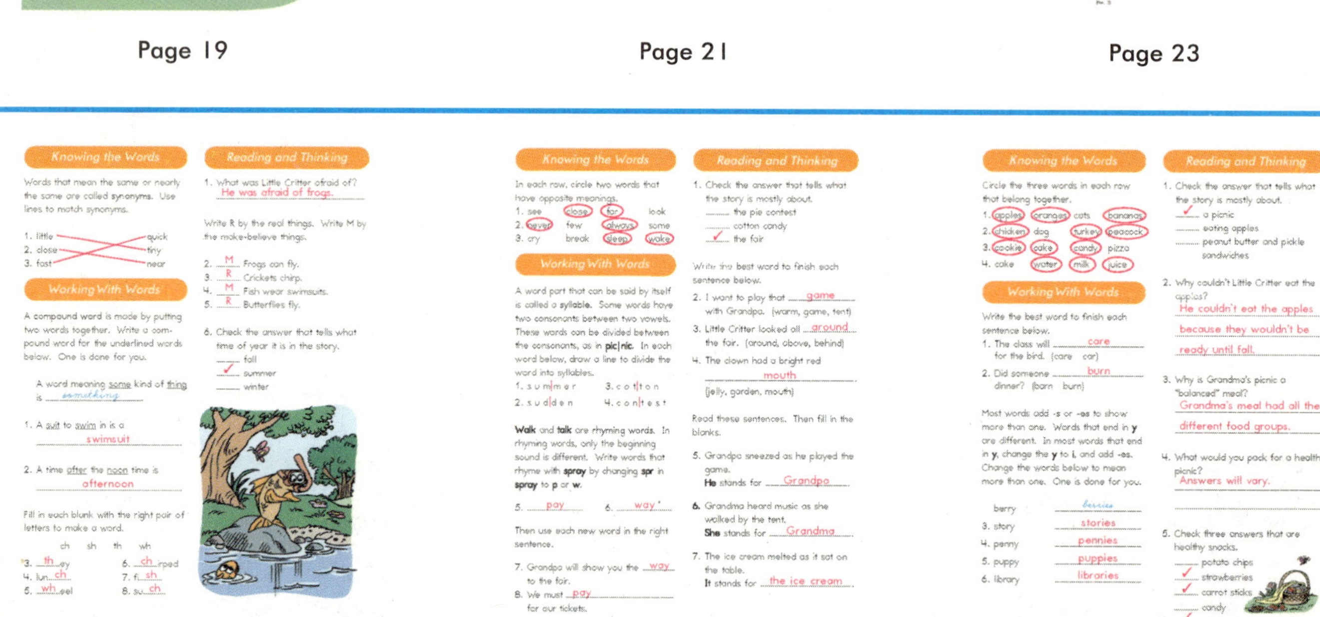

Knowing the Words

Words that mean the same or nearly the same are called synonyms. Use lines to match synonyms.

1. little — tiny
2. close — near
3. fast — quick

Working With Words

A compound word is made by putting two words together. Write a compound word for the underlined words below. One is done for you.

A word meaning some kind of thing is something

1. A suit to swim in is a swimsuit
2. A time after the noon time is afternoon

Fill in each blank with the right pair of letters to make a word.

ch sh th wh

3. th ey 4. lun ch 5. wh eel 6. ch irped 7. fi sh 8. su ch

Reading and Thinking

1. What was Little Critter afraid of? He was afraid of frogs.

Write R by the real things. Write M by the make-believe things.

2. M Frogs can fly.
3. R Crickets chirp.
4. M Fish wear swimsuits.
5. R Butterflies fly.

6. Check the answer that tells what time of year it is in the story.
   - fall
   - ✓ summer
   - winter

Page 25

Knowing the Words

In each row, circle two words that have opposite meanings.

1. see (close) (far) look
2. (never) few (always) some
3. cry break (sleep) (wake)

Working With Words

A word part that can be said by itself is called a **syllable**. Some words have two consonants between two vowels. These words can be divided between the consonants, as in **pic|nic**. In each word below, draw a line to divide the word into syllables.

1. sum|mer 2. sud|den 3. cot|ton 4. con|test

Walk and **talk** are rhyming words. In rhyming words, only the beginning sound is different. Write words that rhyme with **spray** by changing **spr** in **spray** to **p** or **w**.

5. pay 6. way

Then use each new word in the right sentence.

7. Grandpa will show you the way to the fair.
8. We must pay for our tickets.

Reading and Thinking

1. Check the answer that tells what the story is mostly about.
   - the pie contest
   - cotton candy
   - ✓ the fair

Write the best word to finish each sentence below.

2. I want to play that game with Grandpa. (warm, game, tent)
3. Little Critter looked all around the fair. (around, above, behind)
4. The clown had a bright red mouth (jelly, garden, mouth)

Read these sentences. Then fill in the blanks.

5. Grandpa sneezed as he played the game. **He** stands for Grandpa
6. Grandma heard music as she walked by the tent. **She** stands for Grandma
7. The ice cream melted as it sat on the table. **It** stands for the ice cream

Page 27

Knowing the Words

Circle the three words in each row that belong together.

1. (apples) (oranges) cats (bananas)
2. (chicken) dog (turkey) (peacock)
3. (cookie) (cake) (candy) pizza
4. coke (water) (milk) (juice)

Working With Words

Write the best word to finish each sentence below.

1. The class will care for the bird. (care car)
2. Did someone burn dinner? (barn burn)

Most words add -s or -es to show more than one. Words that end in **y** are different. In most words that end in **y**, change the **y** to **i**, and add **-es**. Change the words below to mean more than one. One is done for you.

berry	berries
3. story	stories
4. penny	pennies
5. puppy	puppies
6. library	libraries

Reading and Thinking

1. Check the answer that tells what the story is mostly about.
   - ✓ a picnic
   - eating apples
   - peanut butter and pickle sandwiches
2. Why couldn't Little Critter eat the apples? He couldn't eat the apples because they wouldn't be ready until fall.
3. Why is Grandma's picnic a "balanced" meal? Grandma's meal had all the different food groups.
4. What would you pack for a healthy picnic? Answers will vary.
5. Check three answers that are healthy snacks.
   - potato chips
   - ✓ strawberries
   - ✓ carrot sticks
   - candy
   - ✓ raisins

Page 29

Words You Know

1.	2.	3.
run (sun) fun	friend faster (flower)	big (birds) ball
4.	**5.**	**6.**
(dog) did don't	(pond) play day	(puppy) cup sun
7.	**8.**	**9.**
to too (two)	(fish) frog butterfly	go (game) give
10.	**11.**	**12.**
(hot) not now	goes (grass) good	(three) there them
13.	**14.**	**15.**
yellow (yard) yes	be big (bee)	could come (cold)

Page 30